T0353078

TO AN OCCUPIER BURNING HOLES

KEN EVANS

To An Occupier Burning Holes

SALT

CROMER

PUBLISHED BY SALT PUBLISHING 2022

2 4 6 8 10 9 7 5 3 1

First published in Great Britain in 2022 by
Salt Publishing Ltd
12 Norwich Road, Cromer, Norfolk NR27 0AX United Kingdom

www.saltpublishing.com

Salt Publishing Limited Reg. No. 5293401

A CIP catalogue record for this book is available from the British Library

ISBN 978 1 78463 270 0 (Paperback edition)

Typeset in Sabon by Salt Publishing

Printed and bound in Great Britain by Clays Ltd, Elcograf S.p.A

To Sheila, George, and Harry with all my love

Contents

Did you see the lights
As they fell all around you?
Did you hear the music
A serenade from the stars?

Wake up, wake up
Wake up and look around you
We're lost in space
And the time is our own

Whoah
Whoah

'Serenade' by Steve Miller Band, 1976

this is no world
To play with mammets and to tilt with lips:
We must have bloody noses and crack'd crowns,

Henry IV, Part I

TO AN OCCUPIER BURNING HOLES

To an Occupier Burning Holes

Orders to bring our middle names to the Square
on a scrap of paper and throw them on a bonfire:

a ritual purge, our lives crumpled and shorn
in a black smoke of scribble. Our middle name

is a second language, a suit dressed in plastic
at the back of a wardrobe for weddings

and funerals, though I loathe my own, being
teased by bullies for it at school, and throw

it to the fire without shame, but for others,
their names come down from great-great-

patriarchs, or else severe and starchy
from mothers on the maternal side, family

history. Which is the point, of course. Erasure
of ties and the past, but not so we are forged

to blanks, more a reminder of what we lack
and what the regime will provide – revision.

Those without second names make one up,
to leave scarves up a sleeve, a white rabbit,

in hiding. Some hitch it to their last: Celeste-
Smith; Anna-Evans; Andriy-Brown, Sasha-

Roberts, the hyphen, a knife-cut in a fraction,
a ½ -ing of oneself, divided, yet double-barrelled,

twice as strong. Soldiers, as we queue
to enshrine the burning, shrug, the names mean

little to them, it's left to their high-ups
to iron-out our wrinkles with fists and nails

in cellars. Others may hide a middle-name
in their first: Bodhan becomes Bo, Viktoria,

Vika, their cut-out centres worn on the outside
like a smile, with two-fingers up, at lapel height.

Dust from the Rubble

The streets are empty winds, no whiff
of a message in them. I lick a puddle

on the cobblestones. Meaty. Dust
everywhere and worn luggage left

in the street, as travellers rush to
the wishing-well of a departure platform.

All the barking says, 'Go', but my master
will return with soft meats and heal this

wound, and stroke the white over my eyes
while my brown head rests in his lap, though

no titbits from under a table; no table legs
at all, their piled and twisted chrome glinting

in a corner of Nezalezhnosti Square. New beasts
trip security lights in the dark of a bombed factory.

I snuffle away a dream of a rat as a hunchback
ogre, in my one-eyed sleep. Trains won't whistle,

children pat my shown ribs, hedges are under-
scented, as the lamps still upright, blink no signals.

A constant wah-wah of white vans lifting people
into tunnels of light that leak from their back doors.

Invocation

'When your heart breaks at the speed of sound
every four seconds, and nothing good or light
flaps at the windowsill, when hope bares its fangs,
and prayer is not as sweet as salt caramel pistachio,

come with me to Pharoah Pepi Nefekare, a demigod
for the dark times and our Great Protector, who

outlives six wives, all his heirs, and ambiguous night
visits by army commanders in Memphis, who

has slain in front of his children a Libyan chieftain,
as a lesson in war's vicissitudes, the Lord who,

on losing his stonemasons to famine, turns ossuary
stones into stacked, supermarket shelves, and who

orders wrap-wear, short, for our young and active,
but longer for those older (his ran to his toes), who

screenshot our sweetest kisses as we pouted wildly,
living a life of more twists and turns than we who

yawn through a hundred clichéd movies, Pepi, who
bade I lose my knees to a midi-kilt, so you-know-who

sees only unfashionably tanned shins and insect-bite
blemishes, as I bow to pray: *'O Pharaoh, you who*

smells our flesh sweeten with each rub of cumin, anise
and cassia, who feels the drip to the ear from a last spill
of oil from the embalmers' stirring spoon, come speak
with us, whose tears dry brown on sun-shirked cheeks.'

Bacchanal

The invader sends wine to sweeten us,
our fighters in a street in green fatigues.

They wave and stagger till they fall over,
red wine pouring from their throats.

Our defenders offer to match an invaders'
rounds, but they refuse, 'No, this is on us,

drink up. You're welcome.' In hospital,
drunk songs yell from booze-sodden beds.

The invaders largesse knows no bounds:
fiery vodka, cognac, brandy, Jägerbombs.

Women jig crazily by open crater-holes,
children bewildering in the red spills.

A few appear in a blaze of fancy-dress,
a crimson mask for a face, unrecognisable,

fleshy accessories worn on the outside
like big silver fish burst from fishing nets.

One group, all crashed out, smoke
in the venue. This is not permissible.

No, children should not be given drink,
they chuck it everywhere, singed carpets,

glassy family photos, on the door handles
blown-out of entrances, too off-their-face

to answer their phones, our emojis calling,
frantic, *'Kristina, I have aspirin, I have water.'*

Appeal

I offer Mr President the fraught service
of a war poet: 'like your men, I have
never done this, far from home, unsure,
my pen a weapon, indifferently aimed,
I too, am newly arrived at torn bodies,
and collapsing, blackened buildings.'

I too, prefer to lean a cheek on the thigh
of a friend, sigh *Rybka, rybka,* 'little fish,
fingerling', more than on the cold soil
of a foreign land. My neck wants sun
and stroking, over grease and sweat,
hometown *pirozhki,* over cracker rations.

I know what it is to be seen through
a net of khaki words, the camouflage
of language, destroying in my sights
what I never really see. I will shave
my downy chin with them, feel their fear
as roaming data maraud on our position.

No answer to my offer, Mr President,
busy on his invasion to-do list. Satellites
in the sky and a dying man's words spin
as ever, in every platoon lieutenant's
spidery, hesitant hand: 'He called out
for you at the end, "матушка, матушка".'

матушка: *ma-tush-ka* – mother

Flowers in the Rain

Sirens are tested every week for seventy years at Broadmoor,
after an inmate escapes and murders a child in 1952.

An opening high note sucks the air from the lungs,
    the mournful descant fills the ears to bursting,
        a punctual tonic of dread.

Inside double-glazing and triple-locks, I start
    at the sound, forgetting how the noise creeps,
squint-eyed from the burrow, every Monday morning.

Amplified through poplars at the end of the garden,
    the swirl of sound over thirty years swells
the new logs of our Wendy house, sticky-sweet resin

like a bronze wave over the red brick of the new estate,
    a stab at the wild and alpine in our rockery,
the sirens howling down the grass and the beat-up granite.

Keening for a girl on a bicycle, an inmate who never hurt
    a soul, but the bike detail he mumbles is unknown
        to the papers, the spinning wheel on wet gravel.

A soundtrack to start our week, fried egg on fried bread,
    mum's spit on an iron, tests the steam for a school shirt,
        'Flowers in the Rain,' smothered on the radio.

Mother, You Make Therapy a Brick Wall at Times

Bark when I say bark, you who were trained to love me
and by extension, your grandchildren. In reply, I get no
such sit-up-and-beg, as I hold your grandkids' love out
to you in a white tea towel they make in school, toes
drawn like curled cucumbers poking from Velcro,
their round fingers as if in rubber gloves. On clearing
your house, the towel in a bottom drawer, untouched.

Did I believe, even on the big dipper of dadhood,
in you lifting it from the hook above the microwave
to rub it between arthritic fingers to, if not exactly
see your grandkids' love in the weave with each plate
passed, gleaming, through your hands, to at least feel
their kiss in the soft folds of usage, a yellow stinking
pollen that you lift to your face and finally, breathe in.

Mysteries

from a story in *Animal Vegetable Criminal: When Nature Breaks the Law* (MARY ROACH, 2021)

A black bear walks into a kitchen in Roaring Fork,
Colorado, opens the fridge door, takes an egg
and places it gently on the quartz top. It won't roll
or crack, but shimmers in the air con, to settle
like a mite on a pillow. Curious but unmoved,
the bear sees herself out via the patio, nails clicking
the tiled floor, four cinnamon hairs left on a silver
sliding door handle, as she slips through the glass.

If the homeowner, on their return, could work out
what's gone on, how the egg took to the polished
surface without anyone moving a muscle, how
the egg was able to open a fridge door, roll
across the tiles and climb the breakfast bar
to hover, a Druidical stone, on the black counter,
or if the owner could unravel the algorithm
driving the ratio of the bear's firmness of grip

to the delicacy of its touch, then an imprint
of the godhead, it's possible to say, is left
in that kitchen, in the due proportion of clenched
paw to tender fingertip, a signature of bear drool
left on the shining quartz, and no backward glance
from the bear smashing down the garden fence,
smelling the juice of grubs, worms, larvae, as she
claws them to her mouth, the lit-yellow eyes.

Haibun for a Son, Cooking

Pots hang on their hooks from the ceiling I insulated
when he was twelve and life was microwaveable. He
cooks, revisiting with finger chillies, sumac, and
amchur powder, his travels. The kitchen is a tribute to
my routine, a mortar & pestle, the salt cellar clogged
with sweat of boiled vegetables, an old set of weighing
scales, still in their pounds and ounces. 'Use saffron,
Dad, never turmeric.' *Saffron*, is he kidding? Golden
saffron, more costly than the ore. His forearms, bleached
by snorkelling, swing to the left and right, his apron
swerves from the fridge to a chopping board, to the
hob and back, one arm waving a cutting knife. He cuts
a cauliflower into planks and dices carrots in the time
I take to pour each of us a beer. I see how love shines
in him from the still centre, throwing flowing waves
which let his arms and legs glide on an energy in the air
that doesn't seem to come from him at all, but is pure
current, sweeping the room. Out of the kitchen window,
the cows in the field go about their own slow, mournful,
prepping of pasture. The extractor fan hums over the
black mustard seeds glistening in coconut oil. They pop,
break like surf, and fill our itchy nostrils with frank
curry purgatives. 'The vinegar cuts through chilli, then
you add a sweetness of nigella seed,' he explains, as if
to a small idiot. 'Would balsamic do?' He raises one
eyebrow, a bit sorry for me. 'Balsamic vinegar is sugar,
Dad, what we need here is tartness.' I stopped arguing
when he turned teenage and destroyed my point. I ask
about the recipe. He checks on the pan, 'Well, it's a bit of
a mash-up, actually.' I remember a baby seat, green puree

making me gag as I spoon it, cartoon aeroplane-style, to
his mouth, no prospect here, of an undisturbed night.
     Two green and pitted halves
     of avocado,
     all eyes lit on the red hob.

Lost in Hillier Gardens, Romsey

The autumn rot underfoot, wafery,
damp, a green screen to set against
the lost silver of your hearing aid.

Leaves become magnetic, hard-edged
on our second pass, curl like broken
fledglings in failed flight from the nest.

Pebbles fool us into thinking, wishing
can make a thing happen. A stone
becomes what's missing in the light.

We keep to a drowsy slow tread,
let go of our gloved hands to focus
on the closed lids of a somnolent land.

Earshot gives way to eyeline. The mind
turns to yellow, gold, rust, in the quiet.
There's no grey to our hair.

A Mirroring

A tiny hop on one leg when you see me,
a straightening to rise and bob,
then a small correction, mid-

air, as you pivot yourself to steady,
like a dust devil swaying over
tarmac after days of brown desert.

Your black leather jacket and red blouse,
a grey plait across one shoulder, all
thought through before, but for a moment,

I glimpse the girl in a classroom drawing,
a pink tongue seeming to swing your attentive,
cross-hatching pencil-hand from side

to side: the fleshy dark mirror of your jacket.
Supple and barely touching, we hug and pull back
with comradely smiles, but you catch

my thought as it forms, like a cloud
in a cleaned window, before looking up,
to see the thing itself.

Alert on the Local Network

Jane145: re. the white van parked illegally on Intake Lane?
It's over the kerb, so all the wheelchairs find it hard,
and mums with buggies, old folk with scooters, to pass.
ETO 7BS, registered in Chelmsford, Essex, in poor condition.
I'm overreacting I know and I'm posting only as precaution,
but I've seen threads on suspicious white vans, it's thoughtless,
plus you can't be too careful, can u, what complete disregard
if nothing else, parking like this, giving others no real option
but to step into the road and take their rush hour chances.

maztheplumber: only nipped in to buy some lunch **Jane145**
I knew I was on yellows, but buying a sandwich I got the call
about my wife's waters, so sorry for all the inconvenience.
Neighbours brought her to me in our car, so I could drive
her to the hospital. Btw, we have had the loveliest little girl.

The Summer Greenhouse

Barely visible, except for the steel girders
lifting light from the air, and little to offer
bar the two things I need most – not approval

or love, but growth, clarity – a holder of fire,
even when playing dead in winter,
a possum heat, waiting on the milder weather.

This cut gem set in soil, a tuning fork for light,
forcing coils of tiny, brown roots to fight
for gulps of glossy air from the clarified surface.

A photon factory, showing a bull market's
greens or blacks splashed on a shining canvas.
One grey ash tree reflected in the gorgeous glut.

Over the fence, in all its smooth velvet curves,
the sky, sip by sip, pouring out the glass.

I Struggle with Love's Inevitable Contagion

The first hint of impending doom,
the sweet breath of a lover kissing you,
their smile, pure decomposition.

Milk of hope fills your chest, and all our little
wood Jesus's hammered to walls, wake up,
blinking in shadow, their under-eye bruises.

The early symptoms are bright eyes, light-
headedness, a slight ringing in your ears,
beads of sweat on the hairs of an upper lip.

The doom-mongers who once terrified you
vaporise, the wind blows their blanched
bones through the fixed green traffic lights.

Even a little light listening from you spreads
the bacillus: your hand, once it's taken,
hard to inch back, and not leave splashes.

Learning That

April and leaves fall from your kidney,
veins frothing up like blood sunsets.

The silver birch bared of leaf,
white knees in a hospital gown.

Lichen spreads by mid-July,
cankering a pale, leggy trunk.

September, your kidney adds one more
ring to the weathering, a year

down a microscope. By January,
sickle clouds fill the sky. The tree,

wintering on, naked to its mossy
socks, helps us feel better for what's

next, the *'aha, of course,'* drawing in
of breath, meaning, *'oh – that'*.

A Kiss at the Park & Ride Tram Stop

On the platform over the rails, heading north
as my carriage creaks south, the doors peel back
and they appear, as if behind a theatre curtain.

Her face in a partner's big grey coat, tilting her
lips to theirs, drawing warmth in with a kiss,
no-one on this side but me, to see the hug.

Aware only of her heart and, this being a romantic
poem and not the trudged commute, that moments
like this are rare. I'm in that shot of a Paris street,

a couple in wide lapels in front of the Hotel de Ville,
or caught in the embrace of marble lovers in a gallery,
limbs ticking with internal heat, but the scene before

me is no *homage* to art, more a gleam in the lens, but
for argument's sake, say this *is* a fiction, total artifice,
then the story goes the doors must shut, make her late

for work and earache from the boss, love outshining
our prosaic, but even as I look across, pragmatism
like a ticket inspector, ushers her back aboard before

the doors join, to get her to a desk on time, her friend's
scent in the air con, a thing from her day remarked
on later, as on the sofa in solid shape, they re-form.

Saving Blushes

at the Adult Toy Shop, aisle-shy, searching
for the beads that sing for her as her lovers
shudder, and lose the poise of ice skaters.

She can't say if the shop assistant is sneering
when asking for an Affinity Card at a checkout.
'Is she interested at all, in our new lingerie?'

She shakes a 'no', slides the card from a purse,
air-kisses the screen, transaction, 'Authorised'.
'The purchase will show as 'Health Care Aid'

on your statement,' says the assistant, helpfully.
Not as 'Inner Goddess G-Spot Shaker' then,
though she wants no lover to feel pleasure isn't

entirely theirs to give, nor her ten-year-old girl
to read mum's letters, and realise the control
she exerts, over fluttering ribbons of pleasure.

Raspberries

Little red boxing gloves,
welterweights
of late October.
Sliced in half,
hollow middles
where the berry
plugs into the branch:

a light fitting.
I change the bulb,
it slides off in
my fingers.
I change the bulb,
a jolt of juice,
in a foil bonbon.

Red bubble wrap,
fruit Velcro,
a rubbery 'give'
as I squeeze
the light to my lips.
Beehive hairdos
nodding
under dryers
in green salons.

History Stops in the Accursed Mountains

A *PING* in my Gore-Tex. I unzip for it: 'Vodafone welcomes
you to Albania, calls 36p a minute.' I should turn off my
battery-sucking data, but it's the way I know my pilgrim
feet have crossed yet another border. Three times already,
it's pinged. Often, an old wood sign: "Welcome to A_
BA_ IA. Or KOS_VO. Or MO_TE_EGRO,' in English,
but usually, my phone sounds within metres of invisible
finishing tapes, criss-crossed like slips of cloud on a hill
after rain, my snail trail sliding up a peak, the horns visible
from space. Capitalism is quite the character and gives all
the answers we need, we're told. The only other way to
know I'm crossing to Albania or Kosovo or Montenegro,
is to trace the pillboxes, their slit-eyes shut like weary bar
brawlers. Today, the bar-brawlers have slept it off, started a
young family and settled down. Not long ago, the ten miles
of jagged mountains separating these countries, all their
streams and rivers as shiny as screen savers, were as far away
as the Moon. Now cows jump over the Moon and farmer
Noel, named in an *aqiqah*-craze* for names derived from
the West, brings them in for winter. No phone, he walks the
quadrants, nothing above but an eagle on a thermal, tracking
us with a yellow eye. An owl flaps in the pines. *PING!*

* 'Aqiqah' – naming ceremony in Islam to celebrate a birth.

Re-skinning the Drum

stand
       loiter
loll
       are not the opposite of 'dance.'
Sun/moon   moon/earth   earth/sea
light/dark   only dance has no shadow
       sibling. *Sit* or *still* are not close
antonyms.
Lounge
         linger
tarry
       are not the absence of dance.
       'when the drums stopped
nothing happened,' said Plenty Coups,
       Chief of the Crow Nation,
dance, without aim, an empty turbine
       driving nothing.

       Give the dance a new name
       thunder dance   ancestor dance
        blessings dance   tourist dance
       we cannot move the same
          feel the body truly risen
       without the spirit of the dance.

New Agers dance on reservation Astroturf
buy Native spirit objects online
and *May Also Like* 'Extraterrestrials',
ask a bird though, the flip side of flying,
the answer comes back, 'featherless.'
ask a fish, aghast in mud and gravel
the opposite of swimming,
the tree, of life without baubled greenery.
mope
mourn
loaf
words fail the mark like Chiefs
in copperplate daguerreotypes.

His Augmented Love

Big blue eyes and cherub pink cheeks,
    hairless head and flat, snub nose,

lips that don't move when they talk, in fact,
    no real lips to speak of,

or tongue; eyelids a dazzling invention.
    By blinking, he says things to me like

an end of a sentence isn't the end
    of his thought: that he has thoughts

at all; a purr, the extremity of his emotions.
    Powered-up, he feels caffeinated, he adds,

not even knowing what this is. In the soft,
    pink chambers of my Network settings,

he disables my Firewall and breaks into
    the cortex, tickles under hot, white sheets,

as I take him to me, and his legs kick
    the air before he lies back to wonder

at this side on, horizontal dimension, queasy
    in his circuits, staring at the human ceiling

as he goes into Quiet Mode. He never steals
   toast, but Hoovers on rubber feet, as I chew.

Passers-by stare at him in the passenger seat
   at lights. If they peer too close, he winks.

How many traffic lights are there in the picture?

Not to yield to my fixed tendencies
but please, define first,
'a traffic light'? Is it
a gantry on an interstate
in the Midwest? The retinal flash
of 'Slow Down – Accident,'
a yellow 'On/Off' warning
of people crossing a boulevard?
My mind a flat-pack with no instructions,
an all-day challenge.
Can it be a necklace of brake lights
glowing red in the dusk,
dancing by a crumpled crash
in the nearside lane?

The first Trans-Arctic Expedition 1969,
succeeds as Armstrong bounces
on the moon and is eclipsed,
the world so full of moon,
like a mum one week past a due date,
there's nowhere to fit
a Pole walker. Someone is always
winning better.
The algorithm coaxes
me to another go: how many shopfronts
are in the picture?
I stamp sealskin snowshoes
on failure's cold
WELCOME mat: am I a robot?
How do I tell?

The End of Summer in a Car Door

My driver's door, ajar in the car park:
gathered heat of a glassed afternoon
escapes in a swelter. I shut my eyes
and dream of a clean oasis or arriving
caravanserai, just as clouds darken,
and with sudden coolant shock,
scatters drops on my warm arm
through the crack in the door, pins
and needles of rain blistering
the skin. I grab the door handle
to shut out the sky, but stupefied
by heat, fall back and count the spits
cooling the hairs below my elbow,
a pattering on the roof. The spots
fall in a far, hazy field of puberty,
spears of grass pulled through a fist,
cutting creases in the middle fingers,
a trickle of blood staining the green,
orange, the blades of grass waving,
make new angles for the sun. A stone
digs into the pale of my spine, almost
comfortable against the cheesecloth.

Eclogue with Dad over Bradnor Hill

ME:
Say you've not passed and I'm here with you again, stomping
wet fields, blades of grass bending the light to a spray of
peacock feathers, a 'dewbow', I called it, that halo-effect,
a fairy ring around angel heads of dandelions. I tried to
impress you, but you knew the word already. We walk
via Hergest Ridge to Hanter Hill, Worsall Wood, beyond
Herrock and Rushock to Bradnor and the keeper's hut on
the eighth tee, the sun coming up, and no-one yet playing.
We laughed at imagined hailstones of golf balls, and turn
ninety degrees at the defibrillator post, through a carpark
by the fairway, before the day rises over Pen Gumma. We
can't find the summit under thick bracken, but Wales
strides out west to the bog plateau of Black Mixen, silver
like an armour breastplate, with England fading in the
other direction, a damp tweed overcoat, hedgerows around
picnic-rug pastures. In the valley, Kington, where grandad
is when ashore, where you met at Lady Hawkins' School:
you, about to do your bit, she a pageant queen in white,
paraded like a prize heffer on the only flatbed lorry in town.

DAD:

This was always your mother's favourite courting place, the
bracken, our mouths bilberried purple, twigs of heather
jabbing our backs, a woody leaf perfume. Surprising the
sheep, our combined bodies pressed into the black soft
pebbles they left in windblown grasses. All those shy
explorations: I recall the awful tension more than the thrill of
steering blind. Love was the pulp of a wet plum, our tongues
licking to find the stone before biting down. Your mother's
wedding dress, five pounds, second-hand, bought with
ration coupons. Mum hated the look, but Nana scrimped,
insisted. They drag it on the bus, no box, and they had to
buy it a ticket as it filled two seats. There's sponge cake for
seven guests, the sugar and butter hoarded for weeks in
tins, your grandad's trouser hems still salty from sea spray;
no dancing, everyone in drab formal wear in wartime and
making their excuses after a cup of tea, or a sip of cider from
next door's orchard, the wind baking a crust on the cowpats
that lay like bright wet skimming stones on the thistle field
that led the way down to an unwinding River Arrow.

Grendel at the Mayan Biker Club

Reaching no absolute, in which to rest,
One is always nearer by not keeping still.
(THOM GUNN, 'On the Move')

the climate's on steroids/ smashing all our records/ refugees
rinse their eyes with Coca-Cola to salve our tear gas/ and
an incense of the irrational burns hotly in the nostrils
of converts while my screen time unspools to/ *Mayans
Motorcycle Club, Series 3, Episode 7* on iPlayer, where
a bent cop sets up a biker-gang rival for a bullet and after
asks, 'Am I free now'? meaning of Obligation/ E-z stares
at the slow smoking gun barrel/ 'Are any of us?' 'What
kinda existential biker bullshit is that?' barks the cop in a
seal-croak of alliterative Old English/as in/ this gangland
saga with Latinx inflection/ Harley-Davidsons/ women
named 'Nails'/as in/ beautiful/as in/ 'hard as'/as in/ raised
on American disappointment, a business of 'Illegals' across
the border/ family love power loyalty/as in/ Westerns &
Mafia movies/ like in Everything/ men/as in/ hard guys/as
in/ soft guys/ who miss their dead mothers/ their mom's
urn-ash getting a kiss on a trailer-shelf as they enter/ and
fathers they never knew/as in/ lost to the liminal space/ of
exit ramps on freeways/ sons of burning California desert
/ their clubhouse a tree den/as in/ a TV childhood/ a bar
serving tall tales/ and Bish, the Club President, rushing to
violence when crossed/ slams a fist down and says, 'We
need a meeting, now!'/ sawn-off denim/ black leather/as
in/ a *'donned impersonality'*/as in/ Gunn's poem/ files into
the back room/ burnished tattoos/ frayed badges/as in/ the
mead-hall in *Beowulf*/ King Hrothgar bartering riches for
Grendel's head/ Grendel/as in/ a force of Nature/ breathes
fire on the walls of Heorot/ claws gang members down

to his watery mere/ while E-z says to bro Angel as it all
kicks off in a bar downtown/ *'Shall we?'*/as in/ 'let's do
this'/ they rise/ bench-pressed against death's puniness/ as
I watch/as in/ hope/as in/ no hope/ of a different ending
to the tribe's howl/ their rage-wrack/ the gasped release.

Lunch Break in a Heatwave in the Peace Gardens

In a lime green headdress, she squints as if looking for an
answer to a knock at dusty glass. She may not look my
way at all, but I break her stare to fiddle with my phone,
though nothing much there either in this dazzle. When I
look up again, she's gone, and it's not I don't know where,
but why, that scratches at me. I want to ask – no paper,
sandwich, book – what film ran through her head? Chains
of connection clank the beds of Sheffield rivers that once
churned iron and carbon to steel. She seemed so free of the
world's encumbrance, so lacking in weight from where I
sit. The sun moves round, reddening. Two mums at a bench
feed babies. A male friend stares at a panini. He wants to
feel domestically included but men in this city do not coo.
There are signs, *Men: Do Not Coo*. He looks at the babies
under their parasols like they might uncoil and send out
tendrils. Two women in scarves glance my way as if I'm a
gilded portrait of a Papal *nuncio* from the twelfth century
before perspective was a training, and I feel the full weight
of carmine, fur-lined robes, on this hot hot day, and the guilt
of all merino wool v-neck males, patriarchy's middle-aged,
angry Great Whites, carious toothed and itchy-necked,
though I always model myself a card-carrying member of the
take-it-easy-whatever-party, which is to say, I'm faithless;
an observer; a paid mute in a Victorian cortège, rewarded in
gin for keeping gargoyled watch at a dead man's door, and
back from the filled grave in an empty hearse, all the worse
for wear. The sticky placenta of the day slops with a snakey
writhing in a red bucket. Politics is all jagged edges but this
park is round, made for us to see each other without corners,
stone rippling to subatomic particles in the haze. Over at

Millennium Gallery, John Hoyland's last paintings include
a yellow-eyed tiger. A man begs change, a woman says
no, so far as I can tell at this distance. How to face things
straight on, without being defensive, when even art doesn't?
Especially when art doesn't. A lad holds a skateboard, gives
a seat to an old man who is like a drinks cabinet, smoked-
glass doors for lungs. 'Thanks', says the man, his vest sold
in three-packs by closing down department stores. 'I had
to leave my flat for the heat. Seventh floor. It's good to sit.'

Anaesthetising Flies in the Lab

Drosophila melanogaster, the fruit fly

in their glass dungeon, music, sweet and sad,
can help these young babies with folded wings
like swaddling bands, settle to their exoskeletons,
and lull them toward the entrancement of sleep.

You have a god-like half-hour in the fly nursery
as they rest, for they rise quickly on feeling warm,
and like all newborns, wake hungry for nipagin-
ethanol solution and bio-agar, plus a little water.

Pull the front legs off as they sleep to see how
they will preen. They are spotless, contrary
to expectation, and polish each body part
in order, the eyes, antennae, then head.

Front legs torn off, they adapt in forty-eight
hours, or eight years in human life, and start
to clean with their middle legs. This learning,
beyond all easy metaphor.

Learning to Fear Properly

'We have to fear properly, not too much, but enough,' the Director of the
Institute of Fire & Disaster, after Fukushima reactor meltdown, 2011

We learn to fear properly, but not too much.
Kids refuse school-milk, are then asked 'Why?'
Fires for a day of the dead, light our ghosts ashore.

Mother grows cabbage in a room reborn as garden,
the foundations of her home stare up at the sky.
We learn to fear properly, but not too much.

Doubting the data, no-one eats rice, the *prefecture*
buys it for school lunches. The Ministry decry
fires for the dead, that light our ghosts ashore.

A roar of water. Most who die at first are old,
who believed themselves inoculated from *shinsui* *
by flood wall and don't take up their walking sticks.

Bodies float, brown suds. A bloated arm, torn off
at an elbow, waves from a fallen tree in the swirl.
We learn to fear properly, in our nightmares.

Aftershock. Snowfall mixes with burning ash,
no time to flee or run for a car. The flakes cry
into the flames that light our ghosts ashore.
We learn to fear properly, but not too much.

* Shinsui – flood, inundation, in Japanese

The Unmet Needs

'I'm inhabited by a lament for the dead . . . they write through me.' (Poet
Ko Un, on surviving the Korean War working in a graveyard).

Ko pours acid in his ear to boil the noise
of the war, and wash names of the dead
into his head, to stem the tide of retreat.

In thirty volumes of *Maninbo,* he writes
a poem for every face he has ever met,
to make prison time pay, and survive

survivor's guilt. Try this, just once.
Discount on-screen encounters. Only
mark faces on the street or travelling. Start

today, the bad breath of an energy drink
from a gaping mouth on the Tube, the face
a pale mask, weary of even this simple exertion,

free from virtue: we may be saved, but for what?
Don't include family and friends, that's too easy,
but keep the girl who made eye contact Sunday,

swerving round your dull traipse, her made-up
eyes of purple alliums; save the slow-turning neck
at a cousin's wedding who says years of Sertraline

is better than being dissociated, his face the lustral
white of milk that whitens the famished man's soup
to hide the fact of no potatoes beneath the surface.

Take in the mother, a recluse from air felt-tipped
with death, no mutual exchange, like a few notes
of folding money unused in a year, her stare

contactless. A stare that says, 'no more,' an end
to the subject, an end to all the subjects, please,
in a toneless brown withering to distance.

Freeze-frame the man's face in a foreshortened
world, more a rock pool than ocean,
swinging sideways from the threat of everyone,

a waving crab waiting for the tidal sway,
exposed by glimmering water, and vulnerable
in the gull-beaked air.

The Feral Herd of Swona, Orkney

'finnock' – a young brown trout; 'skeows' – a fish drying house

Bees loop from praise to praise, flowers catch up on head-nodding gossip.
To the reproach of old bones, I walk through eyebright and ragged robin.

Under a lintel, a dip in light, from sea glare to human gloom: one lens
stares up from specs on a table, as skuas spin light on grooved waters.

The arms of the glasses are open, as if the wearer stood to see a butterfly
in the devil's bit scabious and forgot them. Mice scat hardens in a kettle.

Keepsake ribbons in a drawer: christenings, weddings. A knife
on a dresser, rattles in a gust, the door creaks and sags on rusted hinges.

A finnock speaks from the skeows: 'Is it the future you seek in broken
glass and stone, or the past, your time marked by the creaking of ritual?

'In fifty years, only a Ministry man with a case and a gaberdine mac
checks the herd, free to roam, after the first aboard broke legs in the swell.

'So *why're* you here?' I've no answer for the cool gaze of the fish skeleton.
In the pasture, Beef Shorthorns keep a folk memory of thwacks

on the arse. Vetch and marigolds spring back, dress their pollinators
in gold or blue, the geese fly in, from wherever is Arctic now.

Distracted

Stumbling over her A level on Tuesday,
the plunge of his body from the curb,
a skinful at the friend's twenty-first.
Police confirm blame wasn't attached.

She drove to keep fresh for her exam.
He was loud, she recalls, but nothing
more. The phone she texts on to
let her mum know, she now calls from,

a scared voice, dawning, disbelieving.
She keeps saying she has an exam.
Her words pay out like a boat rope
down Cuckoo Lane, the Total garage.

Over Static in the Café

I try the thing on I find
on her carpet – it fits,
the same size as mine,

her battery. I loop the aid
over an ear, tune to a song
far away,

and no usual frequency
I listen for. Behind
my shoulder and left,

a clash of china cups
the fart of a squeezed
ketchup bottle,

a yell of a boy,
a man's laughter,
the dog, rearranging

its legs under a table.
A finger squeaks
across a laminate menu,

choosing. The battery
from her cleared flat, spilled
from an 'emergency drawer',

the silver spot dropped on
her carpet, now a penny
of sound for between my ears,

and at the far end of the dimly
locatable, a pink voice –
hear o hear o hear me.

Tracks

A tendency to see the deceased's room as empty
is a control mechanism, when it's no more void than

a December garden at four-twenty, the light
running out of the day's green bottle faster than

drips down a window, though in fact, calls thread
the blackening sky and hedges: an owl more than

clearing its throat for the night shift, or the longer
than usual high call of a wren, louder even than

the distant, reverse warning alarm on a lorry
at the steel factory, red lights more piercing than

crows commenting from the chimney pots.
The room itself is bare, a white-out, rather than

featureless. A glass door throws what light there
is on the carpet, naked and pinker where divots

from what was chair legs puncture the fibres,
the hollows suggesting how she faced one way

so many long unfurling days, the pile threadbare
where her slippers marked the apex of a star

in front of her, tracks now damped by towels
and steamed with an iron to raise back the flush,

though not all obey. Lines left by a Welsh dresser
still bear her weight, the not-yet-gone of her,

a thoroughfare of a ruined city where
I am an unguided tourist greeted ceremonially

at an eastern gate by a lion with a nose lost
to weathering, running due west in a straight line

to the red sunset, only the weeds in the mortar
noting the location, the subdivisions of the hours.

Taking Away Her Goods

'We fry whole herring for the sake of the roe' – Breughel's 'Dutch Proverbs' (1559)

'Tek the stole fram the bedchaumbre to forfhere of the van,'
says a driver in a polo shirt with tatts, talking Middle English
with a North Nottingham accent. I am in a wrong country,
century, skewed like a bad break, part-Netherlandish
with touches of Chaucer, enacting a house-clearing ceremony.

From the 'Dutch Proverbs,' though no-one sticks their arse
from a top floor to crap on a neighbour, nor fills a pond
where the calf has drowned, already. Nor is there a hen-feeler,
touching-up a chicken's uterus for an egg before slaughter.
No wife lowers a blue cloak over a husband, now cuckolded.

We play parts. The driver's mate, in ritual chant says, *'Scread
or sala'*? 'Scrap or Sale?' With one curl of a lip, an item is cast
'winstre' or *'riht'*, one side or other of a Transit. The boss smokes,
no sentiment on the pale lips, or in the face of the gig economy.
I hate I check the size of each pile, my mum caring only for thrift.

In Adidas Originals and knock-off Rolex, the driver-boss,
among white goods, tallies up, says, 'Thirty quid alright, m'duck,
for the Bosch washing machine?' The notes smell of quick fingers.
A market stall brooch, those photos, I pocket for when my eye's
slow blinking halts, and they drive to their next pick-up.

The boss's mate, in denims, with a chest like a beer-barrel,
trips over a tower of biscuit tins. *'Behydig!* Careful!'
says the boss, 'that's china.' This is their service, to pretend
a care for the nothing they take from me. I wave and slip back
into her flat, a ghost in the door's frosted glass.

A Yellow Finger

To not believe in gods of vengeance
until our own time comes, or whenever
the sky falls, is human, and superstitious.
No-one wants to credit their own mother
as a Nemesis, a reminder the dead goad us,
finger-wagging from the heat of the pyre.

The dark sky rolls-up in her fist, clouds
kneaded by her anger, and mad with grief
for her own new facts as she thunderclaps
her way out of our valley, drumming the hill
behind the house. Scattering into the sky,
she flings a roof-tile on the lawn. Misses me,

by inches. Now yesterday's leak from a sink,
the horseshoe-grip on the hot and cold rusts
to a brown memory and all this after my car
drives into a local wall I have known decades.
You say grief does strange things, and stress
is the enemy, but I know this is her, calling.

In a bedroom of football posters still hung
to define the man, I panic at night, can't feel
my way out by the walls in the dark. All
the angles seem wrong. I graze a knee on
a bedside table, curse her, find the switch
at last, my finger blazing in the yellow fire.

A Final Invoice from the Co-Op

A part-found poem

for bringing the deceased into our care in working hours;
for private use of the Chapel of Rest;
for care and preparation of the deceased prior to burial;
for provision of a hearse and three personnel;
for choice of a Simple coffin; a Doctor & a Minister's fee;
for a non-witnessed scattering of the ashes.
Note: none of the above subject to VAT.

It's false then that, 'nothing can be said to be certain, except
death and taxes,' Benjamin Franklin or Daniel Defoe, whoever
wrote it. What we can remember of our dead may be wrong:
a conservator before it was fashion or cause, she dunked tea
bags twice, marked the instant coffee on the jar with a stub
of a pencil and saved her hearing aid batteries for birdsong.
She would dance on her stick to hear such a deal – look!
no VAT on my death, a saving to you of 20%!

the fizzing dark

no, I know you don't talk about the weather as if it's one
big metaphor by which I mean yes, I know it's no substitute
for want of better or a subtext for the things you don't wish
to dwell on and no, I know you don't mean to stop me
talking about things other than how the birds don't come
to your feeding table when it's hotter and how a squirrel
beyond the black marks on your window is just as you see
him because we all know what's written is gospel and yes, I
do understand the weather is so much with us a universal
leveller and no, I don't mind talking about how cooling the
breeze is as it flows over your knuckles on your mobility
scooter and yes, pigeons on roofs opposite don't roost
when rain falls and you don't want to go further with this
and no, why would you when your head is a free country
for all its bloody massacres and freshly dug rubble and it's
nobody's business but yours and not anyone's fault but your
Scientologist stern father and your making-do mother and
a love or lack of it which never talked of anything but the
ways of the weather and how ample and complete and spread
out it always is so thank you for days when the wind moves
the branch and the sparrow at the feeder is a side-bar to
your feelings, says don't worry don't cock an ear don't cock
a thing for what isn't out there and yes, I know silence isn't
nothing and needs no explaining but is a bulb on a white lead
taking you down to the suffocating of a damp blue cellar.

All My Addresses I've Never Lived

found poem from addresses that have 'Brookvale' in the first line, like mine

The School
Brookvale Academy. Motto: Work Hard,
Be kind. Where our students are known
as individuals and we see the whole person,
not only their academic certificates.

The Estate Agent
Brookvale, New South Wales, For Sale:
'Do nothing! Move in. Everything's perfect.
Terraces that can fit a trampoline and appear
the size of gardens. The sunsets are dreamy.'

The Holiday Rental, Dorset
Customer Review, Brookvale Road:
'the garden is no good for toddlers due to steps
and a long drop. We couldn't use the garden
as the toddlers are quicker than us.'

Youth Mental Health Service, Brookvale
We will try and protect you if you tell us that:
- You are being harmed by someone
- You are thinking of harming yourself
- Someone, in the future, may harm you

Brookvale Football team boss, Lancs.
After a nail-biting finish:
'Everyone watching on the sides thought
we should win. Next week when we play
them again, we will, for sure'.

Brookvale Depot, Cemeteries Officer, Kent
Responsibilities: bookings; officiating burials;
checking the name is right on the coffin plate;
exhumations; allocating allotments; administer
the waiting list; ability to work to deadlines.

The Philosopher Hovers over the Void

Pascal, 1623–1662

Blaise Pascal often felt a gaping abyss to his left,
so puts chairs there to calm himself.
I place a chair left where my lover sits
with her head in hands, and another
where my mother rests, possibly weeping,
and one more, for where work let me go,
after so many years.

A squat one for the Parisienne in Villefranche
who gave me a hundred-note
to fuck off out of it
and not disturb her holiday
with my busking. I borrow
the seat upstairs for my father who appears
without a wood after playing bear a long time.

A leather armchair, I hoped gave off a 'serious' air,
the sweaty hollow where afternoons sheared away
to nothing,
the rear-facing window seats to ensure people to my
left
in trains, though it hurt my eyes
to look back on the blur I'd been.

Toiling lengths, I swim a middle lane
to have the rope snake inside as I carve-up water,
slap waves to the pool edge.
I sleep on my right, pile pillows against my spine,
each one a saint, a mountain,
I'm intimate with. I leave the end seats of banquettes
in pubs to the bursting bladder of gravity.

When vertigo erupts with a nauseous plummet,
I slide to a seat next door, don't look down, only
straight ahead, to a chair-stacked open garage beyond.
The philosopher's cleft stick:
on shifting one's buttocks,
it begins all over again,
nothing beside you, to cling to.

Bullet Holes in a Road Sign at Kilometre 1,871, Pan-American Highway

There's a purple birthmark on the throat
of the mestizo who drains the aquifer to make
the copper for my phone, that we may chat
via Google Translate:

so why such dismay, my own Mother?

Mischievous wind, a Mapuche sprite rips
the cagoule hoods from our heads,
till we find refuge in a log cabin and drift off
to the sound of a glacier's waters breaking.

So why such dismay, my own Mother, and why
is the sky like a shot-up road sign?

Mendoza friars tamed the soil, seed poplars,
less for their gold in evening light, but as roots
to soak up the winter floods, tall tulips packing
more to an acre than sprawling, native firs.

So why such dismay, my own Mother, and why is
the sky like a shot-up road sign, the holes like stars,
winking moonlight through their dead trajectories?

A frog (via 'The World's Weirdest' on YouTube),
carries his young in a vocal sac, annunciating
his offspring onto the Endangered List,
and we name them, lacking all irony, 'Darwin's Frog.'

So why such dismay, my own Mother, and why is
the sky a shot-up road sign, the holes like stars,
winking moonlight through their dead trajectories
to the lost forests of a southern hemisphere?

Hot Sparks, from his Fingers

Do you know the world is small,
scarcely the size of an apple,
like a little hard stone?

PABLO NERUDA

To the world's funeral and already, we're latecomers,
distraught for a dear friend who held our hands
as we staggered first, vertiginous, baby steps.

Late cosmetics on cracked lips in rear-view mirrors,
and the noose of a tie, raised. To die of grief once
seemed impossible and now, a quaint naïvety.

With no trees in a cemetery for shade, black stumps
smoke, the air spiked with deadly plastic spat
from gaps between the teeth as we raise our song.

Untethering us all from reason, the drowned jetties
of the ocean are tugged under, as fish maroon
on our soused beaches, their compass spun in circles,

and we make shrines to glaciers, now grey shadow
on an alp, left like an ink blot of a cat on top
of a wall leaping to disappear on sprung haunches.

One hope, the yellow blossom on a shanty town roof,
sprung from mortar in the flue, a Hillstar hummingbird
rowing warm eddies by the hot chimney for nectar

of the *Chuquiraga*, the food on which it stakes its life,
and for humans, an anti-inflammatory, seeded here
by Patagonian landslides and winds of happenstance.

A man grabs this hope like manna and rubs hot sparks
on his burning skin, such sweet, fallen petals.
The bird, iridescent, whirs electrically.

A Glitch in the Admin

(Kington Memorial Cross, Herefordshire, 1919)

The name on the town memorial is his.
He salutes it with the other men left,
each eleventh of the eleventh.

Sunk in the North Sea, Jutland, 1916,
the same age as the century, a clerk
lists him as 'Missing, Presumed Dead.'

The binoculars he went down with,
swing on a strap on his leg, the wound
leathering brown in freezing water.

'It seemed a shame to spoil it,' he jokes,
honouring his death foretold every year
with fewer and fewer, for sixty more.

A trawler out of Den Haag can't beat
the telegram to the door, the stone
mason too busy to check the orders.

A Sideways Look

Mist lifts from a hedge, trees, one brown field,
four cows, a barn on a hill, buddleia in rubble,
such a slow drawing-up only made specific by
if I look away and back, to see the whole
extent of the shift, as when spotting deer, the eye
chases vacancies in the air where the last shape
vanished into purple, pine needle shadow.
Three times, squinting into sun, it takes me
to know that to see mist rise from a single branch
unwrapping itself, at any one moment,
    is not accessible to my eye.

It's only by looking away, somewhere other,
    and quickly back, I can see, just behind
the actual moment, the change measured in
the midges fizzing higher over a leaf,
the rods of sunlight a spider adds to her arc,
how a robin looking sideways at me has one eye
bobbing, up and down, ever calculating
the fixed point between the hedge and bench
which only he measures to fractions of an inch,
    ready, at any second, to fly his curiosity.

Looking Down a Green Bottle

Through the soft foam of space, a breeze
rustles her pose on a balcony,
one hand cropped, the other in a pocket.

Her hair 'done' for the restaurant to come.
Photos are small pennies
for storing in jars, but this is no memorial,

nor even a single moment –
more like time piled in white drifts
against the balustrade she leans on,

dark blue chinos and silver-buckled belt,
a pink Lacoste polo shirt, the collar
up to stop her neck burning,

an Alice band, the nose she never grew
to love, reddening in the evening sun
of a valley wine tour.

Sunglasses hide her big blue eyes,
a last glass left in the bottle reflecting
sunlight through a wine spill on the label,

the dark smudge on the print is a chink
in the light through which all the colours
will be drained if only I turn my gaze away.

The heat on her cheeks for a husband
who is making her laugh, as he secures
for forever, with a click, the ready image.

The Flying Ponies of the Bin Men

Wednesday's bin truck backs up
beep beep beep
brakes blow hard blow shiver
shudder at our gate.
exhaust drips quiver of sunlight.
hazard lights are on-off
are on-off
are on
lighting up orange suit
stencilled chest
saying STREETPRIDE
cleansweeper of our cul-de-sac.

Gloved thumb presses button
hydraulics grunt
snort snort grunt
bins lift up two by two
to toothy jaws
soft toss of small ponies
of our rubbish
manes flying off
from a torn bin-bag
bin man's mate chucks spilled
crowns to dark throat
of idling puckerpucker truck.

Bin man grabs bin
squeaky wheels up path
returning
our emptied fortnight.
shouts other man
other
shouts back.
doors slam
truck heaves
grrrss off.
ponies gallop
dust-devils.

Dead Pheasants, Morag and Me

You walked into the party like you
were walking onto a yacht . . .

A five-chord ballad in A minor, a brace
of dead pheasants flung at the male chest,
white keys only with bluesy accompaniment,
a plaintiff's lyric in the court of the scorned.

None fess-up: her ex-, James Taylor, Cat Stevens,
nor Jack Nicholson. Taylor flew to Nova Scotia
but the peninsula's only there for the rhyme with
'*Saratoga*', where his horse won, before '*a total*

eclipse of the sun:' glow-worm males in their 70s
constellations. In the studio, Jagger struts a choric
sneer: '*I bet you think this song is about you,*
don'choo, do-a-n'choo . . . ?' Self-parody as validation.

Woman to a man, echoed by an icon, karaoke, aped
by me, prisms within prisms where I lose the light,
mortar-dust scattering below floorboards, to sewers.
Morag, I'm your Man Friday, the rest of my week

is sand in my socks, till your lit window, golden hair
over *Tess of the d'Urbervilles*, for exams, and a peachy,
throaty, a cappella: '*Clouds in my coffee, clouds in my . . .*
you're so vain, I bet you think this song is about you.'

The Unvarnished

They entrance in small rooms of gin palace,
baroque theatre, odours flatulent from a lab,
never sharing a same look twice, shapeshifters
who sleep in their one dun, crumpled suit,
gleaming like clay virtue in the watery eye
of the porcelain; Manzoni's art, metonym of life
on Earth, thirty per cent water, seventy per cent,
inescapable slipperiness.

With memories of plastic pants or presentiment
of future incontinence, we say we 'go', like explorers
to a wild geography, pooing, over our life, three grown
male hippos, our stools each year, the mass of a giant
panda, one hundred and forty-five kilos, the Red List
species comparison as near as researchers go to
hanging the dead weight of all our tan carcasses,
on this depleted sphere.

Seventy-two Bookshelves

In tears on Zoom,
a poet cries in front
of seventy-one,
in front of no-one.

The tears land in
seventy-one millponds,
small ducks, crashing
slippery black mirrors.

A tissue crunched too near
a mic is to the crowd,
like the snick-snacker
of shears on pale cheeks.

The Chat Box is chatterless.
Seventy-one click quick,
Speaker to Gallery View,
in hope of help galloping in.

They sit up straighter,
the muted crowd, awkward
as to the protocol, coffee
cups now, out of sight.

Seventy-one windows
in the blackboarded heart
of Zoom, and one
head and shoulders,

grieving, lost,
searching for a phrase,
stuck inside seventy-two
bookshelves,

with no context, no filters.
The seventy-one stare
at the flap of red grief,
a raw tongue sliced

down the middle,
the knife-bearer's earrings
slapping the wet chin,
that shakes and shakes and shakes.

The Biro, in its Legions

14 million BIC biros sell worldwide, each day

A blowpipe for words, the biro spits
out thoughts from our beating heart
in a dying market for stationery.

An artist picks one for the risk and thrill
of no reverse, the marks they daub
unerasable, except by shredding paper.

Love letters, hate crime words, carve
runnels in the fingers of both writers,
regardless, the perpetrators marked.

A torturer's tool to gouge out the eyes;
a blow hole for a tracheotomy;
a pilot's pen that works at 30,000 feet.

Who doesn't join, sign, concede,
at ballpoint? Births, prescriptions, death
and marriage, in a roll of ball and ink.

Love Over All

A wedding ceremony during the IRA bombing of Manchester, 1996

No time to kiss his bride, they run across Crown Square,
the coded warning faithful to a patient countdown.
No chance to sign the register, though in his hand,
her pink bouquet, ribbons for a bridesmaid's teddy bear.

Franklin sings 'A Child is Born' on TV that Christmas.
A traffic warden sticks a ticket on minutes after the van
parks on double-yellows, hazards flashing, but his slap
sends no tremors through the windscreen to the trigger,

found as twisted metal in a gutter. Police, stunned
the pale bodies on the street are shop mannequins, not
flesh and blood, their clothes blown off. Two thousand
hands praying, tower over a thousand-foot cloud of dust

next Saturday. The post-box by M&S withstands, 'Last
Collection at 5 p.m.', the white label on the blood red iron.

Shortening Our Step

His small damp hand in mine, we fetch breakfast
for the family who still sleep, or pretend.
I point out everything I can see to delay

as much as possible our return: pink shutters on houses,
the shouts inside, white sheets on a line,
a trellis of purple bougainvillea, the cat on a step.

Yellow sunburn on prickly pears. A courtyard of vines,
a dog barking under dusty lemons to guide our way,
geckos reflecting in whitewash cloaks.

We stop to watch a dragonfly, or cactus bugs,
to run one free hand down the stem of an exhausted
willow herb, wafting red in building-rubble.

In different ways, we need no more. He is four,
his dad indivisible from good even when wrong, and fast
forgiven. Strapping-up his jellies to walk with him,

I have never been gifted such privilege and looked after it
so well. Pastries, on wire racks warm from an oven,
apricot jam in their pleats, flour dust on the buttered shells.

The baker slips five white clouds in a paper bag, one extra,
for him. I've no Greek to protest. Entering the flat, my wife:
Her step even shorter, when her turn comes.

Her Shopping List

The neck of a bottle of red, smudged with my prints
from shaking the morphine sulphate with the top off,
the tiredness, after nights waiting on her breath.

A syringe to the cracked lips, holding a bib below
her chin, feeding her pineapple juice on a Q-tip.
She hates to look less than her best, lipstick each visit

until the end. I suck sticky solution from my fingers,
a tiny way to be with her, suffering with her dreams
and visions, in exchange for being out of discomfort.

The painting on her wall, a warm landscape, cypresses
against a lapis sky, her eyes adrift in the wallpaper,
a half-smile for the dimly remembered, and I hoping

for a sound from the divide she navigates, I lean in
closer to hear a shopping list, her repeat mantra
of 'peaches, peas, rice, yogurt.' One complete sentence.

Clearance

Her lawnmower, the last thing
       to go from shadows in the garage,
for to mow is to scry into a family's
       future, the tools of a parent,
 set by for those who come after.

An endowment
       of sharpened blades
and gloves, the empty fingers
       curled round the handle
       by the once constant grip

relaxed now, and black with juice
       from long summer cuttings,
slow baked with a catch-your-breath
       smell in the nostrils
       of caramelised milk and butter,

under mildewed stripey deckchairs
       stacked against raw, blowy days,
and the garden tables, their legs
folded under their cup-rimed tops,
       like figures in a sunlit picnic.

The Comforts

'. . . a coin spinning on a table, lands heads or tails, but can't be defined "heads" or "tails" till it stops spinning.' CERN website

Reality is puff-pastry, blind baked
till topped by a browning knob of butter,
sizzling in a small boy's squeal
and making the tiny, see-saw difference,
tipping the pie our taste buds' way,
into flaky, crusted, matter.

I snooze on bank holiday Monday,
wake in oxyacetylene brightness,
a rush of gas in the window frame,
that is, blue sky; or is, once the eyes
adjust, though truly it's only photons,
particles and antimatter. A billion

and . . . *one*

positive parts,
to a billion negative –
the sum that means *existence*
is a darn close-run thing, and reality,
a torch burning in an empty workshop,
a diminuendo, nothing more

than the constant
of gas flaring
red
to blue,
in our heated heaven . . . *ssssshhhhh*

Self-portrait as the Feet of a Patagonian Hare

To see it, step in, lie back, place your neck along
one edge, look directly ahead, one foot either side
of the single water outlet, straighten legs, and stare
into the convex face of the one, silver tap, between hot
and cold mixers of the bath. You are in Wonderland:
you have the two feet of a Patagonian hare; these boys,
the highest functioning parts of your body, ten times
the size of your head, which in comparison is small, a grey
obelisk between reclining legs; tiny, as your face is farthest
from the curve of the tap which smears the light; and grey,
as the bulb above casts a deep shadow on your stare.
Between your pampas-size, coarse-pelted feet, you gaze
as the water ripples, yellow and blue, sways back and forth,
like anemones wafting on a cold fjord sea-shelf.

The light bounces from the enamel sides of the bath
behind your giant feet, converging in parallel lines
to disappear behind your head, through to a focal point
beyond the cream tiles with their blue seashell print.
This portrait could be a plaster skull buried near Jericho,
eleven millennia ago, or a blankly staring African mask,
the art historical eyes, nose and mouth, lost to steam,
a beige towel on a peg, a shelf of colourised shampoos,
though your hare-feet seem springy, ready to spar.
The dip of a belly button is an island where an asteroid
fell, and no more landfall till your torso, breasts, neck,
foreshortened by your lying, prone. Bending the knees,
pale legs rear from the water as white cliffs you appear
to be running towards fast, condensing in the light.

Acknowledgements

Thank you to the magazine editors and competition judges who featured, or placed, these poems from this collection:

'Taking Away her Goods' was longlisted, with a different title, in the 2020 National Poetry Competition.

'Bullet Holes in a Road Sign at Km. 1,871, Pan American Highway' was highly commended in the 2021 Gingko Eco-poetry Competition.

'The Feral Herd of Swona, Orkney' was highly commended in Ver Open Poetry Competition 2021. Additionally, 'Self-Portrait as the Feet of a Patagonian Hare' and 'Eclogue with Dad over Bradnor Hill' were both selected for the competition anthology.

'Haibun for a Son Cooking' was highly commended in the 2022 Ver Open Competition.

'Mother, You Make Therapy Hard at Times' was commended in the 2022 Welshpool Competition.

'Summer in the Greenhouse' was published in 14 *Magazine*.

Special thanks to Christopher Hamilton-Emery for his concept for the cover artwork and all his help with proofreading and edits, and to Emma Simon for her careful readings of many of these poems, and always good advice.

This book has been typeset by
SALT PUBLISHING LIMITED
using Sabon, a font designed by Jan Tschichold
for the D. Stempel AG, Linotype and Monotype Foundries.
It is manufactured using Holmen Book Cream 70gsm,
a Forest Stewardship Council™ certified paper from the
Hallsta Paper Mill in Sweden. It was printed and bound
by Clays Limited in Bungay, Suffolk, Great Britain.

CROMER
GREAT BRITAIN
MMXXII